E-commerce Marketing Strategies for Beginners

A Comprehensive Guide to Marketing and Selling Products Online

Dr. Miles J. Cooper

Disclaimer

The information provided in E-commerce Marketing Strategies for Beginners: A Comprehensive Guide to Marketing and Selling Products Online is intended for educational and informational purposes only. While every effort has been made to ensure the accuracy and reliability of the content, the author and publisher make no guarantees regarding the results you may achieve from applying the strategies and recommendations outlined in this book.

This book does not offer legal, financial, or tax advice. Readers are encouraged to consult with qualified professionals to address specific business needs, legal requirements, and economic decisions. The author and publisher disclaim any liability for any loss, damage, or negative outcomes resulting from using the information in this book.

Your success in e-commerce depends on various factors, including your skills, resources, and business environment. Results may vary. The content of this book should be used as a guide, not a guarantee of success.

All rights reserved. No part of this publication may be reproduced, distributed, or transmitted in any form or by any means, including photocopying, recording, or another electronic or mechanical method without the prior written permission of the publisher except in the case of brief citation embodied in critical reviews and certain other noncommercial use permitted by copyright law.
Copy right @Dr. Miles J. Cooper

Table of contents

Part 1: Understanding the E-Commerce Landscape

Chapter 1: What is E-Commerce?
Chapter 2: Understanding Your Target Market
Chapter 3: Choosing the Right Platform for Your Business

Part 2: Building A Strong Foundation

Chapter 4: Crafting Your Brand Identity
Chapter 5: Product Selection and Pricing Strategies
Chapter 6: Writing Persuasive Product Descriptions

Part 3: Marketing Your Online Store

Chapter 7: Introduction to Digital Marketing
Chapter 8: Search Engine Optimization (SEO) for E-Commerce
Chapter 9: Social Media Marketing
Chapter 10: Email Marketing Essentials

Part 4: Driving Sales And Building Consumer Loyalty

Chapter 11: The Art of Running Effective Promotions
Chapter 12: Leveraging Consumer Reviews And Testimonials
Chapter 13: Retargeting And Remarketing Strategies
Chapter 14: Building Long-Term Consumer Loyalty

Part 5: Scaling Your E-Commerce Business

Chapter 15: Analyzing Metrics and KPIs
Chapter 16: Expanding Your Product Line
Chapter 17: Exploring International Markets

Conclusion

Part 1: Understanding the E-commerce Landscape

CHAPTER 1: WHAT IS E-COMMERCE?

E-commerce, short for electronic trade, has reformed how organizations and shoppers collaborate. In the digital age, it has become a foundation of global exchange, empowering anybody with an internet association with trade items and administrations on the internet. This section investigates the quintessence of e-commerce, its exceptional development, the opportunities and difficulties it presents, and the different plans of action that characterize it.

Overview of E-commerce and its Development

E-commerce alludes to the trading of labor and products using the internet. It incorporates many exercises, from online retail and digital downloads to monetary exchanges and virtual conferences. The ascent of e-commerce has been filled by mechanical headways, developing consumer conduct, and the global reach of the internet.

The development of online business throughout recent many years has been faltering. In its initial days, internet-based shopping was an original idea, met with wariness by numerous buyers. Be that as it may, the improvement of secure installment entryways, easy-to-use points of interaction, and quick delivery choices changed it into a strong and helpful option in contrast to conventional physical shopping.

By the 2020s, the E-commerce had represented a critical part of global retail sales, and this pattern indicates that things were not pulling back. Promotions, for example, portable trade, voice-actuated shopping, and man-made consciousness-driven personalization keep on pushing the limits of what is conceivable. For fledglings entering this space, understanding its development direction is basic to utilizing the opportunities it offers.

Key Advantages and Difficulties of Selling on the Internet

E-commerce offers a few benefits that make it an alluring choice for business visionaries and laid-out organizations the same:
1. Global Reach
    Not at all like conventional stores restricted by geology, e-commerce permits organizations to take advantage of an overall customer base. Whether you're selling hand-tailored makes or digital programming, the internet disposes of obstructions and interfaces you with consumer s across the globe.
2. Lower Overheads
    Working in an internet-based store commonly requires fewer assets than keeping an actual area. Costs like lease, utilities, and in-store staff are essentially diminished, making it a practical answer for new companies and private ventures.
3. Adaptability and Accommodation

E-commerce works all day, every day, giving customers the opportunity to shop at whatever point they need. This accommodation, joined with highlights like customized suggestions and bother-free returns, upgrades the shopping experience and lifts consumer loyalty.

Notwithstanding its benefits, E-commerce accompanies its portion of difficulties:
1. Extreme Contest
   The simplicity of the section in the online business market has made a jam-audiences space. Standing apart requires a novel offer, powerful marking, and creative marketing procedures.
2. Innovative Conditions
   E-commerce depends intensely on innovation. Issues like site free time, network safety dangers, and installment handling mistakes can upset activities and leverage customer trust.
3. Coordinated factors and Satisfaction
   Managing stock, delivery, and returns productively is a mind-boggling task, particularly for organizations scaling quickly. High delivery expenses or postponements can prompt disappointed customers.
   Understanding these advantages and difficulties assists business people with planning for the real factors of maintaining e-commerce.

Types of E-commerce Business Models
   Online businesses envelope an assortment of plans of action, each fit to various objectives and audiences. Realizing which model lines up with your vision is fundamental for long-term success.
1. Business-to-Consumer (B2C)
   The most well-known E-commerce model, B2C includes selling items or administrations straightforwardly to individual consumers. Models incorporate internet-based retailers like Amazon, design brands like Zara, and membership administrations like Netflix. B2C is great for organizations focusing on enormous, different audiences.
2. Business-to-Business (B2B)
   In B2B E-commerce, organizations offer items or administrations to different organizations. This model is pervasive in businesses like discount, assembling, and programming. For example, an organization giving venture programming arrangements or mass office supplies works under the B2B model.
3. Consumer to-Consumer (C2C)
   Platforms like eBay, Etsy, and Facebook Commercial Center work with exchanges between individual vendors and consumers. C2C models are famous for handing down merchandise, handcrafted things, and specialty items, engaging people to adapt their side interests and abilities.
4. Consumer to-Business (C2B)
   In the C2B model, people offer items or administrations to organizations. Models incorporate influencers offering brand support or consultants giving visual depiction administrations. This model has gotten some decent forward movement with the ascent of the gig economy.

5. Direct-to-Consumer (DTC)

DTC organizations sidestep conventional retail channels to sell straightforwardly to customers through their sites or platforms. This approach permits organizations to keep up with command over marking, pricing, and customer connections.

6. Dropshipping

A quickly developing subset of online business, dropshipping kills the requirement for organizations to hold stock. All things being equal, when a customer puts in a request, the item is delivered straightforwardly from the provider. While it limits forthright expenses, dropshipping requires cautious provider choice to guarantee quality and dependability.

7. Membership Based Online business

Membership administrations give repeating conveyances of items or administrations, frequently at limited rates. Models incorporate dinner units like HelloFresh and excellence boxes like Birch box. This model advances customers unwaveringly and unsurprising income streams.

Every one of these models offers remarkable benefits and difficulties. Choosing the right one relies upon variables like your ideal interest group, assets, and long term objectives.

Online business has changed the manner in which organizations work, offering boundless potential for development and advancement. By understanding its primary ideas — its development, advantages, difficulties, and plans of action — you are better prepared to leave on your journey in this unique field.

CHAPTER 2: UNDERSTANDING YOUR TARGET MARKET

Understanding your objective market is the foundation of e-commerce success. Without a unmistakable brand of your ideal customer, marketing techniques might crash and burn, and you item contributions could come up short. This section dives into the fundamental platforms fo distinguishing your audience, leading compelling market research, and examining custome conduct to guarantee your endeavors align with the needs and preferences of your consumers.

Recognizing Your Optimal Customer

Each fruitful online business starts with a reasonable comprehension of its optimal custome An "optimal customer" the text addresses the gathering, likely discussing the ongoing situation. t purchase your items or administrations. Pinpointing this audience guarantees your marketin endeavors are coordinated effectively and resound profoundly with the perfect individuals.

1. Segment Experiences

Start by characterizing the segment qualities of your likely customers. These may include:
Age: Would you say you are focusing on youthful grown-ups, moderately aged experts, or seniors
Orientation: Is your item focused on men, ladies, or a gender-neutral audience?
Pay Level: What is the buying force of your audience?

2. Psychographic Profiles

Go past socioeconomics to reveal psychographics — what propels your customers, thei qualities, and their way of life decisions. For instance:
-Could it be said that they are earth cognizant?
-Do they esteem extravagance or moderation?
-What leisure activities or interests line up with your items?

3. Personal conduct standards

Understanding how your customers interface with items can give significant experiences:
-Is it true or not that they are successive consumers or periodic consumers?
-Do they favor purchasing on the internet or through portable applications?
-Is it true that they are affected by reviews, limits, or suggestions?

Fostering a definite profile of your ideal customer assists you with making items administrations, and marketing systems that reverberate with your audience, cultivating trust, an driving sales.

Market research Essentials

Market research is a methodical interaction to assemble data about your objective market. It gives the information expected to come to informed conclusions about item improvement, marketing systems, and by and large business tasks.

1. Essential Research

Gather information straightforwardly from your expected customers to acquire firsthand bits of knowledge. Models include:
Reviews: Circulate online studies to pose explicit inquiries about inclinations, needs, and shopping propensities.
Focus groups: Host little gathering conversations to investigate conclusions about your item or administration.
Interviews: Talk straightforwardly with likely customers to jump further into their assumptions.

2. Optional Research

Leverage existing information from strong sources to enhance your discoveries. Models include:
-Industry reports from connections like Statista or IBISWorld.
-Contender investigation through site reviews, internet -based entertainment, and online gatherings.
-Experiences from devices like Google Patterns to distinguish well-known search terms connected with your specialty.

3. Contender Research

Noticing your opposition offers important bits of knowledge into what works and what doesn't in your industry. Examine their:
-Item contributions and pricing techniques.
-Customer reviews to recognize qualities and shortcomings.
-Advertising strategies and internet -based entertainment commitment.

A careful market research process permits you to approve your business thoughts, distinguish holes on the lookout, and design your contributions to address the issues of your audience.

Analyzing Your Customer Conduct

Whenever you've recognized your ideal customer and directed market research, the following platform is to examine customer conduct. This includes understanding how customers communicate with your brand, settle on buy choices, and foster dependability.

1. Following Internet-based Conduct

Leverage devices to monitor how customers explore your site or associate with your brand on the internet. For instance:
-Google Examination: Comprehend where your traffic comes from, which pages are most visited, and how long customers stay on your site.
-Heat maps: Distinguish the region of your site that draws in the most consideration.

-Internet-based Entertainment Investigation: Track commitment measurements like likes, offers and remarks to check revenue.

2. Understanding the Consumer's Journey

The consumer's process is the interaction customers go through while choosing to make a buy. This journey regularly incorporates:
-Mindfulness: The customer distinguishes a need or issue.
-Thought: The customer investigates arrangements and analyzes choices.
-Choice: The customer picks an item or administration to buy.

By planning this journey, you can think up customized systems for each platform, guaranteeing a consistent and enticing experience.

3. Gathering Input

Direct input is significant for understanding customer inclinations and trouble spots. Urge customers to share their contemplations through:
-Post-buy reviews.
-Email subsequent meet-ups.
-Internet-based entertainment surveys or remarks.

4. Recognizing Patterns

Remain on the ball by recognizing designs in customer conduct. Are more customers shopping on cell phones? Do they incline toward eco-accommodating bundling? By recognizing patterns, you can adapt your methods to remain relevant and engaging.

Understanding your objective market is certainly not a one-time task; it requires continuous examination and investigation to adjust to developing patterns and consumer needs. By recognizing your ideal customer, directing careful market research, and investigating customer conduct, you lay the basis for a fruitful online business adventure.

CHAPTER 3: CHOOSING THE RIGHT PLATFORM FOR YOUR BUSINESS

Picking the right online business platform is one of the most pivotal choices for any e-commerce. The platform you select will act as the foundation of your tasks, affecting everything from customer experience to versatility. In this section, we investigate famous platforms, the elements to consider while choosing one, and the underlying moves toward setting up your internet-based store.

Overview of Famous Online Business Platforms

E-commerce platforms offer an establishment for building, making due, and developing your internet-based store. Every platform accompanies special elements and advantages custom-fitted to various business needs. The following are the absolute most famous platforms:

1. Shopify
Best for: Little to medium-sized organizations searching for convenience.
Key Highlights:
-Natural intuitive store manufacturer.
-Mix with numerous sales channels (Facebook, Instagram, Amazon).
-An assortment of applications and modules to improve usefulness.

Downsides: Month-to-month membership expenses and exchange charges on specific plans.

2. Woo Commerce
Best for Organizations previously involved in WordPress or searching for broad customization.
Key Highlights:
-Allowed to introduce (requires facilitating and area costs).
-Profoundly adaptable with subjects and modules.
-Search engine optimization well disposed, utilizing WordPress' abilities.

Disadvantages: Requires specialized information for arrangement and support.

3. Amazon
Best for: Business visionaries needing admittance to a gigantic customer base.
Key Highlights:
+Openness to a huge number of dynamic consumers.
-Satisfaction by Amazon (FBA) for strategies and delivery.
-Confided in standing for believability.

Downsides: High rivalry and vendor charges.

E-Commerce

4. BigCommerce
Best for: Scaling organizations with complex item inventories.
Key Elements:
-Inherent Search engine optimization devices and marketing highlights.
-No exchange charges on any arrangement.
-Adaptable framework for developing organizations.

Downsides: Higher beginning expense contrasted with different platforms.

5. Etsy
Best for: High quality, one-of-a-kind, or specialty item merchants.
Key Elements:
-Low forthright expenses.
-A devoted audience for inventive items.

Disadvantages: Restricted customization and high exchange charges.

Key Elements to Consider: Spending Plan, Adaptability, Highlights

Choosing an E-commerce platform requires a cautious assessment of your business needs and objectives. Consider these variables while settling on your choice:

1. Budget

Evaluate both forthright and continuous expenses, including membership expenses, exchange charges, and additional items.
-Figure extra expenses for facilitating, area enlistment, and installment passages if material.
-Guarantee the platform accommodates your monetary arrangement without compromising fundamental elements.

2. Versatility

Pick a platform that develops with your business. For instance, assuming that you expect to increment product offerings or global extension, the platform ought to oblige these changes.
-Assess server limit, and customization choices, and update pathways for future requirements.

3. Convenience

Think about your specialized skill. Platforms like Shopify and Etsy are easy to understand while WooCommerce and Magento might require coding knowledge.
-Try out preliminary renditions or demos to guarantee you're open to exploring the platform.

4. Customization Choices

E-Commerce

Decide to what lengths control you will go for over the plan and usefulness of your store. Platforms like WooCommerce and BigCommerce offer broad customization, while less complex platforms like Etsy are more prohibitive.

Elements and Instruments

Search for fundamental elements like versatile responsiveness, stock administration, installment entryways, and advertising combinations.
Concentrate on platforms that have integrated website design tools to enhance your store's search engine visibility.

Customer service

Strong customer service is fundamental, particularly assuming that you are new to e-commerce.
Check the platform's accessibility of live talk, email support, or committed account directors.

Market Arrangement

Guarantee the platform lines up with your specialty. For example, Etsy takes care of innovative vendors, while Amazon suits mass-market items.

Setting Up Your Internet-Based Store

Whenever you've picked the right platform, now is the ideal time to set up your internet-based store. While explicit advances might shift relying upon the platform, the general cycle incorporates:

1. Enlisting a Space Name

Pick a space name that mirrors your brand and is not difficult to recall. For instance, if your brand is "EcoLux Pags," a site like www.ecoluxbags.com would work well. admirably.
Use domain registrars like GoDaddy, Namecheap, or the platform if it provides hosting services.

2. Choosing a Template or Theme

Settle on an expert and responsive plan that lines up with your marking.
Guarantee the format is dynamic, as numerous customers shop through cell phones.
Tweak tones, text styles, and format to keep a steady brand character.

3. Setting Up Installment Passages

Incorporate installment choices like PayPal, Stripe, or Master card handling.
Offer various installment techniques to take care of assorted customer inclinations.

4. Adding Items and Classifications

E-Commerce

-Transfer great pictures for every item.
-Compose convincing item portrayals that feature elements and advantages.
-Arrange items into classes for simple route.

5. Arranging Transportation and Assessment Settings
-Characterize your transportation approaches, including costs, conveyance times, and transporte choices.
-Set up charge rates in light of nearby regulations and guidelines.

6. Testing Your Store
Prior to going live, test your site completely.
-Check for broken joins, slow stacking times, and any specialized errors.
-Guarantee the checkout cycle is smooth and secure.

   Picking the right platform is an urgent choice that will shape your online business development and usefulness. By understanding the highlights, restrictions, and remarkabl qualities of every platform, you can settle on an educated decision that lines up with you objectives. When your foundation is set up, the subsequent platform is to zero in on creating area of strength for a character, which we'll cover in the accompanying part.

Part 2: Building a Strong Foundation

CHAPTER 4: CRAFTING YOUR BRAND IDENTITY

A strong brand personality is a foundation of progress in e-commerce. It characterizes how your business is seen, separates you from contenders, and fabricates an association with your audience. In this section, we investigate the significance of marking in e-commerce, the components that make a noteworthy brand, and strategies to fabricate entrust with your customers.

The Significance of Marking in E-commerce
In the crowded universe of online retail, marking is something beyond a logo or a slogan — it's the quintessence of your business. It shapes how customers see your items, associate with your business, and recollect your store long after they buy.
1. Separation in a Serious Market
With a huge number of online stores, marking recognizes your business. A strong brand personality enhances your store's significance and allows you to stand out in a niche market.
2. Customer Reliability and Trust
A strong brand makes a profound association with customers. At the point when individuals feel they can believe your brand, they are bound to return and prescribe your items to other people.
3. Expanded Apparent Worth
A successful brand can legitimize premium evaluation when customers associate your brand with quality, expertise, or exclusivity, they are willing to pay more.
4. Marketing Effect
Marking gives a steady message across the entirety of your marketing channels. Whether through internet-based entertainment, email, or promotions, a strong brand personality intensifies your effort endeavors.

Instructions to Make a Critical Brand Name, Logo, And Message
Creating your brand identity expects consideration regarding a few components. Each assumes a part in forming how customers see your business.
1. Picking a Brand Name
Straightforwardness is Vital: Select a name that is not difficult to spell, articulate, and recollect. Keep away from excessively complicated or conventional names.
Pertinence to Your Specialty: Your name ought to indicate what your business offers. For example, "GreenCraft Supplies" signals eco-accommodating making materials.
Uniqueness: Guarantee your name isn't excessively like contenders or existing brand names. Use instruments like Google or USPTO's brand name search to really look at accessibility.

2. Planning a Logo

Visual Straightforwardness: A decent logo is spotless, versatile, and conspicuous initially Consider notable logos like Nike's swoosh or Apple's apple.

Variety Brain research: Pick colors that resonate with your brand values. Blue conveys trust green reflects an eco-kind disposition, and red proposes fervor or desperation.

Consistency: Utilize your logo reliably across your site, bundling, and marketing materials to fabricate acknowledgment.

3. Making a Brand Message

Characterize Your Motivation: What does your business rely on? For instance, an economical dress brand could underscore "design with an inner voice."

Engage Your Audience: Use language that resonates with your ideal customer. If you sell wellness gear, your tone should be energetic and persuasive.

Feature Your Incentive: Obviously, state what makes your business interesting. For instance, "High quality, natural skincare for touchy skin."

Building Trust with Your Audience

Trust is the underpinning of online sales. Customers are bound to purchase from organizations they see as tenable and strong. This is the way to lay out trust:

1. Proficient Internet architecture
-Utilize a perfect, easy-to-understand design with the natural route.
-Guarantee your site is versatile and responsive, as a huge part of internet-based shopping occurs on cell phones.
-Show clear and itemized item depictions, pricing, and transporting approaches.

2. Customer Surveys and Testimonials
-Urge fulfilled customers to leave positive surveys on your site or outsider platforms like Google or Trustpilot.
-Include testimonials unmistakably on your landing page or item pages to assemble social confirmation.

3. Secure Installment Choices
-Utilize secure installment doors like PayPal, Stripe, or Amazon Pay to console customers that their monetary data is protected.
-Show trust identifications (e.g., SSL declaration symbols) on your checkout page.

4. Straightforward Policies
-Obviously frame your return, discount, and transportation strategies. Straightforwardness diminishes dithering and assembles customer certainty.
-Incorporate a FAQ segment to proactively address normal worries.

5. Reliable Communication
- Answer immediately to customer requests and grievances through email, visit, or virtual entertainment.
- Customize your communication where conceivable. Address customers by name and designer reactions to their interests.

6. Refining Your Brand
- Share your story: How did your business begin? What are your qualities?
- Use in the background content to exhibit your group, item creation cycle, or organization culture.
- Draw in with your audience via internet-based entertainment by answering remarks and beginning discussions.

Making a convincing brand character is something beyond configuration work — it's tied in with making an association with your audience and conveying your business' novel worth. With a distinct brand name, logo, and message, combined with endeavors to fabricate trust, you'll establish a strong starting point for long term success.

CHAPTER 5: PRODUCT SELECTION AND PRICING STRATEGIES

Choosing the right items to sell and setting cutthroat costs are urgent to the outcome of your online business. The items you pick decide your specialty, draw in your main interest group, and impact your productivity. Likewise, evaluating systems leverage customer insight, sales volume and edges. This part directs you through the most common way of choosing beneficial items figuring out pricing models, and situating your items on the lookout.

Choosing Beneficial Items to Sell

The groundwork of any online business lies in the items it offers. Recognizing the right items guarantees a consistent interest, lines up with customer needs, and improves your market intensity

1. Distinguish Market Patterns and Requests

Research Industry Patterns: Use apparatuses like Google Patterns, Statista, and social media platforms to monitor arising item drifts.

Break down Contender Contributions: Take a gander at what fruitful contenders are selling and distinguish holes you can fill.

Irregularity Mindfulness: Consider whether the item is popular all year or during explicit seasons. For instance, occasion embellishments top during specific months, while wellness stuff could have a steady interest.

2. Take care of an Issue or Satisfy a Need
-Items that take care of explicit issues frequently draw in a devoted customer base.
-For instance, ergonomic office seats turned into a hit during the ascent of remote work since they tended to comfort issues for locally situated experts.

3. Assess Net revenues
-Compute potential overall revenues in the wake of representing creation, delivery, and advertising costs.
-Use apparatuses like benefit mini-computers to guarantee your item evaluation considers manageable development.

4. Think about Operations and Adaptability

Center around items that are not difficult to store, boat, and handle, particularly assuming you're beginning little.

Assess whether the product offering can grow with correlative things. For example, a merchant of reusable water jugs could add eco-accommodating lunchboxes or compact utensils.

5. Test Your Item Thoughts
-Begin little by obtaining a restricted amount or dropshipping to test interest.

Use pre-request campaigns to check interest prior to resolving to full-scale creation.

Understanding Pricing Models

Pricing is something other than relegating a dollar worth to your items. An essential choice adjusts your expenses, market assumptions, and saw esteem.

1. Cost-Based Pricing

This strategy includes computing the complete expense of delivering an item and adding a markup to guarantee productivity.
Example: On the off chance that an item costs $10 to fabricate and you add a half markup, your selling cost would be $15.
Benefits: Basic and guarantees cost recuperation.
Hindrances: Doesn't consider contender pricing or customer eagerness to pay.

2. Esteem Based Pricing

This model depends on the apparent worth of an item to the customer. High-esteem items can order greater costs.
Example: A hand tailored craftsman neckband might have a creation cost of $30 however offer for $150 because of its special craftsmanship.
Benefits: Permits premium pricing for novel items.
Detriments: Requires profound comprehension of customer insight.

3. Contender Based Pricing

Costs are set in view of contenders' contributions in a similar market.
Example: On the off chance that your rivals sell a comparative item for $25, you could value yours somewhat lower or higher, contingent upon separation.
Benefits: Keeps you cutthroat on the lookout.
Drawbacks: May prompt cost wars or decreased overall revenues.

4. Mental Pricing

This procedure utilizes pricing to impact customer conduct, for example, setting costs at $19.99 rather than $20.
Example: Packaging items at a limited rate or offering free transportation for orders above $50.
Benefits: Empowers bigger buys and rehash customers.
Inconveniences: Can bring down apparent worth whenever abused.

The most effective method to Position Your Items On the lookout

Situating your items includes characterizing how they are seen by customers and guaranteeing they hang out in a cutthroat scene.

1. Highlight Unique Selling Points (USPs)

E-Commerce

-Obviously convey what makes your item unique and significant.
-For example, on the off chance that you sell natural skincare, underline the utilization of normal fixings and eco-accommodating bundling.

2. Leverage Proficient Photography
-Great pictures are fundamental in e-commerce since customers can't see or contact the item.
-Show various points, way-of-life pictures, and close-ups to fabricate trust and convey quality.

3. Utilize Clear and Descriptive Titles
-Item titles ought to incorporate fundamental subtleties like brand, type, size, and key highlights
-Example: "Tempered Steel Protected Water Container - 20 oz, Sealed, Sans BPA."

4. Offer Various Costs
-Give layered choices to speak to a more extensive audience. For instance, offer norm, premium and exclusive variants of an item.
-This permits you to catch customers with fluctuating budgets while boosting sales.

5. Group Items
-Make groups to build the typical request esteem. For example, a "Midyear Outing Set" could incorporate a cooler sack, reusable utensils, and eco-accommodating plates.
-Packaging likewise permits you to sell sluggish things as a part of a bundle.

6. Incorporate Customer Reviews and Testimonials
-Positive reviews and testimonials support believability and impact buying choices.
-Incorporate star appraisals and statements unmistakably on your item pages.

7. Offer Assurances or Returns
-A problem-free merchandise exchange consoles customers and diminishes dithering.
-The state ensures "100 percent fulfillment or your cash back" to energize buys.

Item choice and pricing procedures are fundamental parts of building a fruitful e-commerce By thoughtfully selecting items that meet customer needs, using key evaluation models, and effectively positioning your offerings, you can boost sales and increase profits.

CHAPTER 6: WRITING PERSUASIVE PRODUCT DESCRIPTIONS

A very much-created item portrayal is the scaffold between your item and your customers. It features your item's highlights, interfaces with your audience's requirements, and eventually convinces them to make a buy. A strong item portrayal isn't just about posting subtleties — it's tied in with recounting a story, making emotional connections, and building trust. In this section, we'll investigate the specialty of composing convincing duplicates, the harmony among elements and advantages, and how to enhance your depictions with keywords for better visibility.

The Art of Writing Compelling Copy

The language you use in your item depictions can dazzle or repulse expected customers. Connecting with, a powerful duplicate can separate your brand in a cutthroat market.

1. Understand Your Listeners' Perspective
   Comprehend the inclinations, problem areas, and wants of your interest group.
For instance, on the off chance that you're selling child items, guardians are possibly searching for security, solace, and dependability. Use language that tends to those concerns straightforwardly.

2. Compose as though You're Conversing with a Companion
   Take on a conversational tone that feels congenial and interesting.
Rather than expressing, "This seat is ergonomic," say, "Envision sitting easily the entire day with a seat intended to help your stance."

3. Utilize Tactile and Clear Language
   Help customers envision and feel the item through your words.
For instance, rather than "delicate cover," state "a richly delicate cover that envelops you by warmth and solace."

4. incorporate Narrating
   Make situations where the item tackles an issue or improves the customer's life.
For example, "Ideal for occupied mornings, this espresso creator brews your number one cup in less than five minutes, so you can begin your day empowered and on time."

5. Be Real and Straightforward
   Keep away from overhyping or overstating your item's characteristics.
Construct trust by speaking the truth about what your item should or shouldn't do.

Highlight Features and Benefits

E-Commerce

A typical error in item portrayals is zeroing in exclusively on highlights without tending to how those elements benefit the customer. While highlights depict the item, benefits answer the inquiry, for what reason would it be advisable for me to mind?

1. Grasp the Distinction
-Highlights: Qualities or details of an item.
-Benefits: The positive results or worth the customer gains from those highlights.

2. Transform Highlights into Advantages
Rather than posting, "Produced using tempered steel," make sense of, "Sturdy hardened steel development guarantees this container opposes imprints and goes on for quite a long time."

3. Use List items for Lucidity
-Feature key highlights and advantages in a simple to-examine design.
-For instance:
-Twofold-protected walls keep drinks hot for 12 hours.
-Airtight top for wreck-free transportability.
-Eco-accommodating plan diminishes single-utilized plastic waste.

4. Address Customer Problem areas
-Distinguish Potential Challenges your customers encounter and position your item as the arrangement.
-For example, "Express farewell to tangled links with our minimal, remote charging cushion."

Using Keywords for Better Internet Index Visibility
Enhancing item depictions with the right keywords is fundamental for guaranteeing your items show up in pertinent online quests.

1. Research Significant Keywords
Use devices like Google Watchword Organizer, SEMrush, or Ubersuggest to track down keywords that your main interest group is looking for.
Center around long tail keywords that catch explicit inquiries, for example, "strong climbing rucksack for ladies" rather than just "climbing knapsack."

2. Incorporate Keywords Normally
Stay away from watchword stuffing, which can cause your portrayals to feel constrained and inauthentic.
Place essential keywords in the item title, the initial not many sentences of the portrayal, and list items.

3. Leverage Synonyms and Related Terms

Use varieties of your keywords to catch a more extensive audience. For example, assuming that your essential keyword is "remote headphones," additionally incorporate expressions like "Bluetooth headphones" and "cordless earphones."

4. Upgrade for Voice Search

With the ascent of voice-initiated gadgets, incorporate conversational expressions that customers could utilize while looking verbally.

For instance, rather than "best spending plan cell phone," use "What's the best reasonable cell phone for under $300?"

Formatting Tips for Clarity and Commitment

The construction of your item depictions "assumes a crucial role" in keeping customers locked in.

1. Utilize Short Sentences and Sections

Try not to overpower readers with blocks of text. Keep passages brief and forthright.

2. Separate Text with Subheadings

Use subheadings to sort out data and make it simpler for customers to find what they're searching for.

3. Incorporate Visual Components

Where conceivable, match portrayals with excellent pictures, infographics, or recordings that exhibit the item in real life.

4. Add a Call to Action (CTA)

End your depictions with an unmistakable and convincing CTA. For example:
- "Request now and experience unrivaled solace!"
- "Add to your truck today and appreciate free transportation!"

Composing enticing item depictions requires a blend of innovativeness, vital reasoning, and customer getting it. By refining language, emphasizing benefits, and enhancing website design strategies, you can create representations that engage, inform, and convert.

Part 3: Marketing Your Online Store

CHAPTER 7: INTRODUCTION TO DIGITAL MARKETING

Digital marketing serves as the foundation of a successful online business. It envelops every one of the internet-based systems used to draw in, connect with, and convert customers. In the present cutthroat commercial center, understanding the fundamentals of digital marketing is pivotal for directing people to your internet-based store and expanding sales. This part investigates the essential components of digital marketing, the significance of utilizing different channels, and how to define sensible and noteworthy marketing objectives for your business.

Overview of Digital Marketing Channels

Digital marketing includes different channels, each offering novel ways of interfacing with your audience. Choosing the right blend of channels relies upon your objective market, item type, and business goals.

1. Site improvement (Search engine optimization)
-Internet optimization includes upgrading your site and content to rank higher on internet indexes like Google.
-Benefits: Expanded natural traffic, cost-viability, and long-term visibility
-A pet inventory store can use keywords like "best dog rope" to attract potential customers seeking similar products.

2. Pay-Per-Click Marketing (PPC)
PPC campaigns display ads on search engines or social media platforms, and you only pay when someone clicks on your ad.
-Benefits: Prompt visibility, profoundly designated traffic, and quantifiable return on initial capital investment.
-Example: Utilizing Google Advertisements to advance an occasional deal on winter clothing.

3. Social media Marketing
Platforms like Instagram, Facebook, and TikTok give chances to connect with customers through natural posts and paid promotions.
-Benefits: Brand mindfulness, customer cooperation, and viral marketing potential.
-Example: Sharing customer created content, for example, photographs of customers utilizing your items.

4. Email Marketing

E-Commerce

Email stays one of the best channels for sustaining leads and empowering rehash buys.
Benefits: Direct communication, personalization, and high return for capital invested.
Example: Sending elite limits to endorsers of drive traffic during a blaze deal.

. Content Marketing
Content marketing includes making significant, applicable substance to draw in and hold customers.
Benefits: Assembles trust, instructs customers, and lifts Internet site design enhancement endeavors.
Example: Composing blog entries on points like "10 Ways to pick the Ideal PC Pack."

. Member Advertising
Collaborating with influencers or offshoot advertisers to advance your items for a commission.
Benefits: More extensive reach, low forthright expenses, and admittance to specialty markets.
Example: Teaming up with a movement blogger to advance your baggage assortment.

The Significance of Multi-Channel Marketing

In the present digital scene, depending on a solitary marketing channel restricts your compass and diminishes the potential for development. Multi-channel advertising guarantees you're meeting customers where they are, offering different touchpoints to draw in and convert them.

. Expanded Visibility
By utilizing various platforms, your brand turns out to be. more conspicuous and open to a different audience.
Example: Running Facebook promotions close by a Google Promotions crusade guarantees you catch both social and search traffic.

. Further developed Customer Experience
Customers interface with brands through different channels, from social media to email. -Giving a consistent and steady experience improves fulfillment and trust.

. Enhanced Chance
Depending too intensely on one platform can be dangerous, particularly assuming that calculation changes or market patterns diminish its viability.

. Improved Information Assortment
Each channel gives special bits of knowledge into customer conduct, inclinations, and necessities, empowering you to refine your systems.

Putting forth Marketing Objectives

E-Commerce

Powerful digital marketing begins with clear, noteworthy objectives. Without characterize goals, you risk fooling around and assets on strategies that don't convey results.

1. Define Your Targets
Normal E-commerce marketing objectives include:
-Expanding site traffic.
-Further developing change rates.
-Building brand mindfulness.
-Growing an email supporter list.

2. Utilize the Savvy Structure
-Shrewd objectives are Explicit, Quantifiable, Reachable, Pertinent, and Time-bound.
-Example: Rather than "I need more sales," put forth a Shrewd objective like, "Increment online sales by 20% inside the following three months through designated internet-based entertainment promotions."

3. Focus on in light of Your Business Platform
-For new stores, center around building brand mindfulness and producing introductory traffic.
-For laid-out stores, focus on customer maintenance and advancing change rates.

4. Apportion Assets Wisely
-Recognize the spending plan, instruments, and colleagues expected to accomplish your objectives.
-Example: Assign 40% of your spending plan to PPC advertisements and 30% to content creation assuming your center is traffic development.

5. Track Progress Consistently
Use examination instruments like Google Investigation, Facebook Bits of Knowledge, an email advertising dashboards to monitor your exhibition.

Best Practice for Beginners in Digital Marketing
Beginning with digital marketing can feel overpowering, however zeroing in on key standards will get you in a good position.
1. Begin a Little and Scale
Start with a couple of channels that line up with your audience's inclinations, and extend as you gain certainty and assets.
2. Focus on High-Effect Exercises
Center around techniques with the potential for the best return for money invested. For instance, upgrading item pages for Internet optimization or running a designated email mission can convey huge outcomes.

3. Remain Customer Driven

Continuously consider how your advertising endeavors serve your audience. Draw in with their requirements, inclinations, and feedback.

4. Test and Trial

Run A/B tests for promotions, email campaigns, and site components to recognize what turns out best for your audience.

5. Continue to learn

Digital advertising is continually developing. Remain refreshed with industry patterns through internet sites, online courses, and online courses.

Digital marketing is the foundation of E-commerce success. By understanding different channels, embracing multi-channel techniques, and laying out clear objectives, you can actually drive traffic, draw in customers, and increment sales.

CHAPTER 8: SEARCH ENGINE OPTIMIZATION (SEO) FOR E-COMMERCE

Search engine optimization (SEO) is a crucial mainstay of any E-commerce system. It guarantees your internet-based store is noticeable to potential customers when they look for items or administrations on internet indexes like Google. Not at all like paid promotions, Search engine optimization centers around driving natural traffic, offering a long-term and savvy method for developing your business. This part jumps into the fundamentals of Internet site design enhancement for e-commerce, covering on-page and off-page methods, item page advancement, and techniques to rank higher in indexed lists.

On-Page and Off-Page Search Engine Optimization Basics

Search engine optimization can be comprehensively isolated into two classes: on-page Internet site design enhancement and off-page Internet optimization. Both are basic for further developing your site's internet crawler rankings.

ON-PAGE Internet optimization

On-page Internet optimization alludes to enhancing individual pages to make them more internet crawler-agreeable.
1. Keyword Research
Recognize the inquiry terms your ideal interest group is utilizing.
-Apparatuses like Google Keyword Organizer and SEMrush can assist track down applicable keywords with high inquiry volume and low rivalry.
-Example: For a business that sells eco-friendly water bottles, target keywords like "best reusable water bottles" or "eco-accommodating hydration arrangements."
2. Meta Labels
-Enhance title labels, meta depictions, and header labels to incorporate your objective keywords.
-Example: A title label like "Shop the Best Reusable Water Containers for a Manageable Way of Life" draws in clicks and further develops rankings.
3. Content Improvement
-Make top caliber, instructive, and drawing in satisfied that consternates your keywords normally. Keep away from keyword stuffing, as it can hurt rankings.
-Example: Compose blog entries like "5 Motivations to Change to Eco-Accommodating Water Jugs" to draw in and teach possible customers.
4. Mobile Enhancement
-Guarantee your site is dynamic, as a critical piece of internet-based shopping is finished on cell phones.

OFF-PAGE Internet site design enhancement

Off-page Search engine optimization centers around building your site's power through outer elements.
1. Backlinks
-Backlinks from legitimate sites sign to internet search tools that your internet site is strong.
-Example: Collaborate with influencers or bloggers who can review your items and connect to your internet page.
2. Social Signs
-Dynamic commitment via internet-based entertainment platforms can by implication work on your Internet optimization by driving traffic and producing backlinks.
3. Brand Notices
-At the point when different sites notice your brand, even without an immediate connection, it can help your internet-based power.

Optimizing Item Page Items Internet indexes

Your item pages are the core of your E-commerce store. Enhancing the guarantees, show up in query items when potential customers search for items like yours.
1. Item Titles
-Utilize enlightening and keyword-rich titles that convey what the item is.
-Example: Rather than "Upscale Container," use "24 oz Treated Steel Reusable Water Jug - Eco-Accommodating and Sans BPA."
2. Great Pictures
-Utilize clear, high-goal pictures with engaging alt text for openness and Search engine optimization benefits.
-Example: Alt text like "Blue 24 oz hardened steel reusable water bottle" assists internet crawlers with ordering your pictures.
3. Nitty gritty Depictions
-Compose special, drawing item depictions that feature key elements and advantages.
-Incorporate keywords normally and underline what makes the item important to the customer.
4. Customer Reviews
-Encourage satisfied customers to leave reviews. These build trust and contribute to new, user-generated content on your site, which search engines prefer.
5. URL Structure
-Utilize short, elucidating URLs that incorporate keywords.
-Example: www.mystore.com/eco-accommodating water-bottles.

The Most Effective Method to Rank Higher in Google Searches

Positioning high in Google Look includes executing reliable and vital endeavors. Here are noteworthy platforms to work on your visibility:
1. Center around Customer Experience (UX)
-A quick, simple to-explore site further develops customer fulfillment and diminishes skip rates.

E-Commerce

-Streamline page load times by compacting pictures and utilizing effective facilitating arrangements.

2. Consistently Update Content

-Keep your site new by adding new blog entries, refreshing item portrayals, and presenting new items.

3. Leverage Local Internet site design enhancement

-Assuming that you work locally, streamline your Google My Business profile and remember local keywords for your substance.

4. Utilize Organized Information Markup

-Add pattern markup to your site to give internet indexes extra data about your items, like costs reviews, and accessibility.

-Example: Google can show your item as a rich bit, expanding navigate rates.

5. Build Internal Links

-Connect related pages inside your site to further develop routes and convey page authority.

-Example: Add joins from your blog entries to item pages to urge users to shop.

6. Support Social Sharing

-Add share buttons to your item pages and blog entries. Social signs can by implication help your rankings by driving traffic and commitment.

Best Practices for E-Commerce Internet Optimization

Internet site design enhancement success requires a long-term, steady strategy. Follow these prescribed procedures to fabricate major areas of strength for:

1. Monitor Investigation

Use devices like Google Examination to follow your site's presentation and distinguish regions for development.

2. Target Long-Tail Keywords

Center around unambiguous, less cutthroat keywords that draw in exceptionally designated rush hour gridlock.

-Example: "Best sans BPA water bottle for explorers" is more viable than "water bottle."

3. Improve for Voice Search

The ascent of shrewd aides like Alexa and Siri, streamline regular language inquiries.

-Example: Incorporate expressions like "What's the best eco-accommodating water bottle?" in your substance.

4. Keep away from Copy Content

Guarantee each page has novel substance to stay away from punishments from internet search tools.

5. Remain Refreshed on Internet site design enhancement Patterns

-Internet site design enhancement calculations are continually developing. Continue learning and adjusting to keep up with your rankings.

-Commerce

Dominating Search engine optimization for E-commerce can change your store's visibility and productivity. By executing these strategies, you'll be better prepared to draw in top notch rush our gridlock and convert guests into steadfast customers.

E-Commerce

CHAPTER 9: SOCIAL MEDIA MARKETING

Social media marketing has changed the manner in which E-commerce organizations reach and draw in with their audience. Platforms like Facebook, Instagram, TikTok, Pinterest, and Twitter (presently X) give unrivaled opportunities to feature your items, associate with expected customers, and drive sales. This section investigates the basics of internet -based entertainment marketing, from picking the right platforms to making connecting with content and utilizing paid ads to intensify your range.

Picking the Right Platforms

Every social media platform takes care of an unmistakable audience and fills explicit needs. Choosing the right platforms for your business guarantees that your marketing endeavors reverberate with your ideal interest group and augment returns.

1. Facebook
-Ideal for organizations focusing on an expansive segment, especially grown-ups matured 25-65
-Highlights like Facebook Commercial center, Gatherings, and Promotions Director make adaptable for e-commerce marketing.
-Example: A home merchandise store can make drawing in item exhibits and use Facebook Gatherings to encourage a local area of fans.

2. Instagram
-Visual-driven and well known among more youthful audiences matured 18-35.
-Highlights like Stories, Reels, and Shopping make it a force to be reckoned with for item revelation and sales.
-Example: A style brand can post stylishly satisfying pictures and leverage powerhouse organizations for item advancement.

3. TikTok
-Zeroed in on short, captivating recordings, TikTok is ideally suited for arriving at Gen Z and twenty to thirty year olds.
-Viral patterns and difficulties can assist brands with acquiring gigantic openness.
-Example: A skincare brand can make speedy instructional exercises or take part in moving difficulties to feature its items.

4. Pinterest
-Known for its outwardly rousing substance, Pinterest is great for specialties like home styling, layout, design, and Do-It-Yourself.
-Example: A specialty supplies business can post bit by bit instructional exercises connected straightforwardly to item pages.

5. Twitter (X)
-Best for ongoing updates, declarations, and participating in moving subjects.
-Example: A tech device store can utilize Twitter to feature item dispatches and answer customer questions quickly.

Making Engaging Content That Drives Traffic

Internet-based entertainment success relies on satisfied that catches consideration and energizes association. This is the way to make content that lines up with your brand and charms your audience:

1. Exhibit Your Items

-Utilize top notch pictures and recordings to feature your items.

-Example: A gems brand can share close-up shots of rings and pieces of jewelry, matched with narrating subtitles about their craftsmanship.

2. Share in the background Content

-Adapt your brand by showing individuals, cycles, and energy behind your items.

-Example: A hand tailored cleanser business can post recordings of the creation cycle, featuring its distinctive nature.

3. Teach Your Audience

-Give significant hints, instructional exercises, or industry experiences connected with your items.

-Example: A wellness gear store can share exercise recordings utilizing its items.

4. Leverage Customer Produced Content

-Urge customers to share their encounters and label your brand.

-Example: A dress brand can repost customer photographs wearing their outfits, making social verification and building local area.

5. Draw in with Intelligent Elements

-Use surveys, tests, and question stickers to ignite communication and assemble bits of knowledge.

-Example: A drink organization can request that supporters vote on their #1 flavor through a survey.

Utilizing Paid Advertisements to Boost Sales

While natural substance is fundamental, paid social media promotions can essentially intensify your span and drive designated traffic to your store.

1. Figure out Your Audience

-Use platform examination and experiences to recognize key socioeconomics, interests, and ways of behaving.

-Example: A pet stock store can target promotions to pet people in light of their pursuit history or online way of behaving.

2. Make Convincing Promotion Creatives

-Configuration outwardly engaging advertisements with clear informing areas of strength for and to-activity (CTAs).

-Example: A wonder brand can run video promotions displaying item changes with a CTA like "Shop Now."

3. Retarget Site Guests

-Retarget individuals who visited your site however didn't make a buy.

-Example: A furniture store can show promotions to customers who deserted their trucks including the particular items they saw.

4. Explore different avenues regarding Promotion Formats

-Test different promotion types, like merry go round advertisements, video advertisements, and Stories advertisements, to see what reverberates with your audience.

-Example: A movement gear brand can utilize merry go round promotions to show different items similar to baggage sets and travel embellishments.

5. Monitor and Optimize Campaigns

-Consistently investigate promotion performance measurements, like navigate rates (CTR) and return on promotion spend (ROAS). Adjust the focus on either creatives or budgets based on the specific situation.

Best Practices for Social Media Marketing

To prevail in social media marketing, consistency and credibility are critical. Take on these prescribed procedures to fabricate areas of strength for:

1. Post Reliably

-Keep an ordinary presentation plan to keep your audience locked in.

-Utilize virtual entertainment the board devices like Cushion or Hootsuite to design and mechanize posts.

2. Answer Remarks and Emails

-Effectively draw in with adherents to assemble connections and encourage trust.

-Example: A skincare brand can answer questions about item fixings or utilization tips.

3. Remain Authentic

-Exhibit your brand's novel character and values. Customers reverberate with veritable and straightforward brands.

4. Monitor Patterns

-Take part in pertinent patterns or viral difficulties to remain noticeable and appealing.

-Example: A café can join a moving hashtag crusade like #LatteArtChallenge.

5. Team up with Influencers

-Collaborate with influencers who line up with your brand's specialty and values.

-Example: A wellness brand can work with a famous coach to advance its stuff or enhancements.

Measuring Internet-based Entertainment Success

Last, assess the adequacy of your internet-based entertainment endeavors by examining key performance markers (KPIs):

1. Commitment Rate

-Measure likes, remarks, offers and saves to check how well your substance reverberates.

2. Traffic and Conversions

-Track how much traffic your virtual entertainment drives to your site and the number of those guests convert into customers.

3. Followers Development
Monitor how your audience develops over the long run, yet center around higher standards without compromise.

4. return on initial capital investment on Paid Promotions
Investigate whether your promotion spend converts into significant returns.

By decisively utilizing social media, your online business can areas of strength for assemble mindfulness, drive traffic, and convert easygoing programs into steadfast customers.

CHAPTER 10: EMAIL MARKETING ESSENTIALS

Email marketing stays one of the best and cost-productive strategies for online business organizations. With a typical profit from speculation (return for money invested) of $36 for each dollar spent, it offers an immediate line of communication with potential and existing customers. This part investigates how to construct an email list, create high-changing emails, and computerize campaigns to support commitment and drive sales.

Building an Email List

Your email list is an important resource for interfacing with your audience and cultivating long-term connections. Developing this rundown requires vital preparation and offering certified worth to expected endorsers.

1. Make Alluring Lead Magnets

Offer free assets, limits, or elite substance in return for email recruits.

-Example: A dress store can offer a 10% markdown on the main buy to customers who join their mailing list.

2. Use Pick in Structures in a calculated manner

Put pick-in structures noticeable on your site, including the landing page, blog entries, and checkout pages.

-Example: A Marvel brand can incorporate a spring-up structure offering free examples for email recruits.

3. Leverage Social Media

-Advance your email list on friendly platforms by featuring its advantages.

-Example: A wellness gear store can share a post about selective exercise tips accessible just to endorsers.

4. Gather Emails Offline

-Assemble email addresses during face-to-face occasions or store visits.

-Example: A bread shop can urge customers to join their pamphlet for refreshes on occasional treats and recipes.

Composing High-Changing over Emails

Whenever you've constructed a rundown, the subsequent platform is making emails that resonate with your audience and drive activity. Viable email composing requires an equilibrium of personalization, worth, and lucidity.

1. Create Engaging Subject Lines

The headline decides if your email gets opened. Make it brief, convincing, and applicable.

-Example: "Last Possibility: half Off Deal Closures This evening!"

2. Customize Your Emails

Utilize the beneficiary's name and designer the substance in light of their inclinations or past way of behaving.

Example: A internet-based book shop can send customized suggestions in view of past buys.

- Center around Worth

Feature benefits rather than highlights, and guarantee each email offers some incentive to the user.

Example: A movement organization can share methods for pressing productively while advancing travel frill.

- Utilize Clear Calls to take action (CTAs)

Incorporate a solitary, conspicuous CTA directing users toward a particular activity, like visiting our store or reclaiming a markdown.

Example: "Shop Now and Save 20%!"

- Incorporate Visuals Decisively

Utilize excellent pictures and designs to make your emails outwardly engaging without overpowering the message.

Robotizing Your Email Lobbies for Effectiveness

Automation is a distinct advantage for email marketing, permitting you to send opportune, important emails without manual exertion.

- Welcome Emails

Computerize a progression of welcome emails to present your brand and guide new endorsers toward their most memorable buy.

Example: A pet stock store can send an email with a welcome message, tips for new pet people, and a rebate on their most memorable request.

- Deserted Truck Emails

Recuperate lost sales by helping customers to remember things left in their trucks, offering motivating forces to finish the buy.

Example: "Your number one thing is pausing! Complete your buy now and appreciate 10% off."

- Post-Buy Subsequent meet-ups

Send emails saying thanks to customers for their buy, giving request refreshes, and recommending reciprocal items.

Example: A tech store can suggest embellishments for an as-of-late bought PC.

- Re-Commitment Campaigns

Contact inert endorsers with alluring offers or selective updates to reignite their advantage.

Example: "We miss you! Return and appreciate free delivery on your next request."

- Occasional and Special Campaigns

Plan emails around occasions, sales occasions, or item dispatches to drive traffic and sales.

Example: A home stylistic layout store can advance occasion-themed assortments through an outwardly engaging email series.

Best Practices for Email Marketing Success

- Portion Your Audience

E-Commerce

Partition your email list into portions in view of conduct, inclinations, or socioeconomics to send exceptionally designated emails.
-Example: A design retailer can make separate lobbies for people's assortments.
2. Keep a Reliable Timetable
-Consistently send emails without overpowering your supporters. Week-by-week or fortnightly emails frequently function admirably for e-commerce organizations.
3. Guarantee Portable Responsiveness
-Configuration emails to look perfect on cell phones, as most customer's browse emails on the telephones.
-4. Monitor and Optimize Performance
-Track measurements like open rates, navigate rates (CTR), and transformation rates to distinguish what works and work on future campaigns.
5. Remain Agreeable
-Follow email marketing guidelines, for example, the CAN-SPAM Act, by including a withdrawal connection and trying not to delude headlines.

EMAIL Advertising Apparatuses FOR E-commerce
A few platforms can assist you with dealing with your email crusades effectively:
1. Mailchimp
-Easy to understand and ideal for independent companies beginning with email marketing.
2. Klaviyo
-Custom-made for E-commerce, with hearty division and mechanization highlights.
3. Consistent Contact
-Offers amazing customer service and devices for making outwardly engaging emails.
4. Active Campaign
-Gives progressed mechanization and CRM highlights for scaling organizations.

Measuring Email Marketing Success
Track and investigate these critical measurements to guarantee your email crusades are viable:
1. Open Rate
-Measures the level of beneficiaries who open your emails. Go for the gold above 20%.
2. Click-Through Rate (CTR)
-Demonstrates the level of beneficiaries who click on a connection inside the email. A higher CTR reflects connecting with content and clear CTAs.
3. Change Rate
-Tracks the number of beneficiaries that total an ideal activity, like making a buy, in the wake of tapping on your email.
4. Unsubscribe Rate
-Monitor the quantity of individuals quitting your rundown to measure how well your substance lines up with endorser assumptions.

E-Commerce

By dominating the basics of email marketing, you can encourage further connections with your audience, increment sales, and keep up with customer dependability.

Part 4: Driving Sales and Building Consumer Loyalty

CHAPTER 11: THE ART OF RUNNING EFFECTIVE PROMOTIONS

Making Compelling OFFERS

Promotions are a foundation of e-commerce success, offering a method for tempting customers, increment transformations, and lift sales. Nonetheless, the way to running viable promotions lies in making offers that your audience sees as genuinely compelling.

1. Figure out Your Customer's Necessities

The groundwork of any effective advancement is figuring out your main interest group. Recognize what your customers esteem most — whether it's sans limits transportation, selective packages, or restricted time admittance to premium items. By adjusting your proposals to their inclinations, you increment the possibilities of commitment and transformation.

2. Make a Feeling of Selectiveness

Selectiveness drives activity. Phrases like "individuals just deal," "early access," or "celebrity limits" make desperation and cause customers to feel exceptional. Use apparatuses, for example, devotion projects or email endorser advantages to offer restrictive arrangements to your most connected with audience.

3. Leverage Limits in a calculated way

While limits are successful, they ought to be utilized cautiously to try not to degrade your items. Zero in on:

-Rate Limits: Offering 20% off on buys over a specific sum.
-Level Dollar Limits: A proper rebate like $10 off orders above $50.
-Get One-Get-One (BOGO): Energize mass buys with "Purchase 1, Get 1 Free" offers.

4. Add Worth Through Packaging

Packaging items can build the apparent worth of your proposal while moving more stock. For example, on the off chance that you sell skincare items, pack a chemical, lotion, and sun screen at a marked down cost. Guarantee the investment funds are obvious to the customer, underlining the advantages of the bundle.

5. Incorporate Free Delivery

Delivering costs are in many cases a boundary to online buys. Offering free delivery on orders over a specific sum empowers higher spend as well as disposes of this trouble spot, making the checkout interaction smoother.

Occasional and Holiday Advertising Strategies

Occasional and holiday promotions are chances to benefit from expanded shopper spending. Legitimate preparation and performance can boost these pinnacle shopping periods.

1. Prepare for Significant Shopping Occasions

Occasions like the biggest shopping day of the year (Black Friday), The Monday following Thanksgiving, and Christmas are vital to your yearly sales system. Begin arranging a very long time ahead of time, and construct energy through mysteries and early access offers.

2. Adjust to More Modest Occasions

Past significant occasions, profit by specialty events like Valentine's Day, Mother's Day, or even industry-explicit days. Tailor your promotions to the subject of the occasion, utilizing merry symbolism, duplicate, and item determinations.

3. Leverage Restricted Time Offers

Direness drives activity. "Streak sales" and "24-hour bargains" can set off motivational buys. Use commencement clocks on your site to make a visual sign of the proposition's cutoff time, improving the probability of transformation.

4. Work together with Influencers

Occasion promotions get some forward movement when supported by forces to be reckoned with. Their believability and reach can intensify your occasional campaigns, particularly when their audience lines up with your objective market. Offer them selective markdown codes or early admittance to advance your sales.

Utilizing Shortage and Desperation to Drive Sales

Shortage and direness are mental triggers that persuade customers to rapidly act. When executed legitimately, these strategies can essentially support sales.

1. Feature Low Stock Levels

Show emails like "Just 5 remaining in stock" or "Restricted amounts accessible." This passes restrictiveness and urges customers to act before the item runs out.

2. Time-Restricted Limits

Sales that lapse inside the space of hours or days brief quick choices. Utilize clear cutoff times in your email crusades, site standards, and virtual entertainment posts.

3. Pre-orders and Shortlists

For selective or new item dispatches, utilize pre-orders or wish lists to generate excitement. Customers who feel they're getting early access are bound to buy, particularly assuming amounts are limited.

4. Retarget Deserted Trucks with Criticalness

If a customer leaves their truck, circle back to an email helping them to remember the restricted time offer or looming stock consumption. This delicate product frequently persuades reluctant consumers to finish their buy.

Monitoring and Optimizing Promotions

Running an advancement doesn't end once it's live. Checking its exhibition and making changes continuously are fundamental to accomplishing the greatest effect.

1. Track Key Measurements

Dissect measurements like active visitor clicking percentage (CTR), change rate, and return on promotion spend (ROAS) to gauge the outcome of your advancement. Devices like Google Examination or platform explicit dashboards (e.g., Shopify, Amazon) give bits of knowledge into customer conduct during sales crusades.

2. A/B Test Your Campaigns

Explore different avenues regarding various forms of your promotions to figure out what resounds most with your audience. Test varieties in offer sorts, informing, visuals, and suggestion to take action (CTAs) to refine future strategies.

3. Accumulate Customer Feedback

Post-advancement overviews can give important experiences into what your audience enjoyed and what they felt was deficient. Utilize this feedback to work on your next crusade.

4. Reinvest in What Works

Center around techniques that yield the most significant yields. If your audience answers well to free transportation or BOGO bargains, apportion more assets to those strategies later on.

Building Long-term Worth Through Promotions

While promotions are much of a time momentary procedure, their effect can make enduring impacts whenever executed nicely.

1. Energize Rehash Buys

Incorporate motivators like coupons or markdown codes for future buys in the bundle or affirmation email. This keeps customers returning even after the advancement closes.

2. Construct Your Email Rundown

Use promotions to catch customer data. Offer limits in return for pursuing your pamphlet and utilize this rundown to support leads with future offers.

3. Fortify Brand Faithfulness

Reliably conveying esteem through very coordinated, smart promotions entrusts and fortify your relationship with your audience. Faithful customers are bound to impart your brand to other people, enhancing your compass naturally.

By carrying out these techniques, promotions can turn into an incredible asset for driving sales, building customers unwaveringly, and laying out your brand as a go-to decision in the e-commerce scene.

CHAPTER 12: LEVERAGING CONSUMER REVIEWS AND TESTIMONIALS

Customer reviews and testimonials are among the most amazing assets in e-commerce. They assist with building trust, further develop transformation rates, and improve your brand's validity. In this section, we investigate techniques for empowering reviews, managing feedback, and showing testimonials.

Empowering Blissful Customers to Leave Surveys

Building a vigorous assortment of customer surveys requires proactive systems that connect with and boost your audience.

1. Ask brilliantly

Timing is basic while mentioning reviews. Connect when customers have had sufficient opportunity to encounter your item. For instance:
Send a subsequent email seven days after conveyance.
Incorporate a survey demand with your item bundling.

2. Work on the Review Cycle

Make it simple for customers to leave surveys. Utilize direct connections, QR codes, or bit-by-bit directions to direct them to the survey page. The less advances, the better.

3. Offer Motivations

While motivations like limits on future buys can empower surveys, and guarantee they consent to platform approaches (e.g., Amazon denies boosted reviews except if expressly permitted). For autonomous stores, little signals like coupons or steadfastness focuses can inspire customers.

4. Use Post-Buy Communication

Digital emails, instant emails, or application warnings can be successful updates for customers to share their feedback. Customize these emails to make them captivating.

5. Leverage Social Media

Urge customers to share their encounters on friendly platforms. Featuring customer-created content can draw in additional surveys while helping your internet-based presence.

Managing Negative Feedback Expertly

Negative surveys are inescapable, yet dealing with them really can transform a likely misfortune into a chance to exhibit your obligation to consumer loyalty.

1. Answer Rapidly and Obligingly

Recognize negative feedback expeditiously and keep a quiet, proficient tone. This shows that you esteem your customers' viewpoints and will address their interests.

2. Take the Discussion offline

For complex issues, give an immediate email or telephone number to secretly determine the matter. This forestalls further open disappointment and takes into account more customized help.

3. Offer an Answer

Whenever the situation allows, answer, like a substitution, discount, or rebate on a future buy. Customers are bound to refresh their reviews on the off chance that their interests are settled agreeably.

4. Gain from Input

Negative surveys frequently feature regions for development. Utilize this feedback to refine your items, administrations, or cycles.

5. Banner Unseemly Reviews

On the off chance that a survey disregards platform rules (e.g., contains hostile language or misleading cases), report it for expulsion. This guarantees your input segment stays believable and proficient.

Showing Testimonials to Build Validity

Positive testimonials can fundamentally improve your brand's standing and impact expected consumers. Introducing them decisively is critical to boosting their effect.

1. Highlight Testimonials Conspicuously

Place surveys and testimonials in high-visibility regions, for example,

-Item pages: Incorporate star appraisals and bits of customer input close to the item depiction.

-Landing page: Feature top surveys or customer examples of overcoming adversity to make serious areas of strength for an impression.

-Checkout pages: Show positive reviews to console reluctant consumers and decrease truck surrender.

2. Utilize Visual Components

Incorporate photographs or recordings with testimonials to make them more interesting and legitimate. For example:

-Feature pictures of customers utilizing your item.

-Feature video testimonials from fulfilled consumers.

3. Make a Testimonials Page

Commit a page on your site to feature definite surveys, customer examples of overcoming adversity, and contextual investigations. This concentrated strategy fabricates entrust and furnishes forthcoming consumers with extra data.

4. Leverage Social Confirmation Across Channels

Expand the compass of your testimonials by sharing them via virtual entertainment, email pamphlets, and ads. Labeling customers (with their consent) can build commitment and realness.

5. Feature Explicit Advantages

Coordinate testimonials by key elements or advantages your customers appreciate. For instance:

-Quality: "The texture is delicate and tough, precisely the thing I was searching for."
-Customer support: "The group settled my issue in under 24 hours. Incredible help!"

The Effect of Reviews on Buy Choices

Customer surveys impact purchasing choices more than most advertising endeavors. Understanding their effect can assist you with streamlining your survey system.

1. Fabricate Trust and Believability

Consumers frequently trust peer reviews more than brand information. An item with various positive surveys makes certainty and consoles consumers of its quality.

2. Further develop Search Rankings

Surveys add to site improvement (Internet optimization). Internet crawlers like Google and platforms like Amazon reward items with regular and top-notch surveys by positioning them higher in query items.

3. Increment Change Rates

Showing surveys and testimonials can essentially support change rates. Indeed, even items with a blend of positive and impartial feedback frequently beat those without any surveys whatsoever.

4. Improve Straightforwardness

Straightforwardness constructs trust. By showing both positive and negative surveys, you exhibit realness and an eagerness to address customer concerns.

5. Cultivate Customer Dependability

Empowering surveys gives customers a voice, causing them to feel esteemed and appreciated. This feeling of association cultivates long-term dependability.

Ways to Keep a Strong Review Strategy

1. Routinely Update Reviews

Items and administrations advance. Urge new surveys to reflect current contributions, guaranteeing potential consumers see the most applicable input.

2. Monitor Review Platforms

Remain dynamic on platforms like Google Reviews, Trustpilot, or Amazon. Answering surveys — positive and negative — shows commitment and customer care.

3. Show Success

Celebrate survey success, for example, "1,000+ Cheerful Customers," to create a feeling of believability and success.

4. Work together with influencers

Empower forces to be reckoned with or industry specialists to survey your items. Their support can convey a huge load to your interest group.

By utilizing customer surveys and testimonials successfully, you can lay out trust, help sales, and construct long-term brand devotion in the cutthroat online business scene.

CHAPTER 13: RETARGETING AND REMARKETING STRATEGIES

Retargeting and remarketing are fundamental strategies for amplifying customer commitment and supporting sales in the e-commerce space. These techniques center around reconnecting with potential consumers who have connected with your brand but haven't yet changed over into customers. This section investigates the essentials of retargeting and remarketing, techniques to execute them successfully, and devices to accomplish quantifiable outcomes.

Figuring out Retargeting Promotions

Retargeting is a procedure that includes showing promotions to individuals who have visited your site or connected with your substance yet left without finishing a buy. The objective is to keep your brand on top of the brain and urge them to return and change over.

1. How Retargeting Functions

Retargeting depends on following devices like treats or pixels. At the point when a guest peruses your site, these devices secretly record their way of behaving, permitting you to serve fitted promotions to them later.

2. Advantages of Retargeting

Higher Transformation Rates: Retargeting draws in potential customers who are now acquainted with your items, making them bound to buy.
-Brand Review: Persistent openness to your brand keeps your items in the front of the consumer's psyche.
-Cost-Viability: Retargeting centers around warm leads, decreasing the expense per securing contrasted with focusing on chilly audiences.

3. Kinds of Retargeting Promotions
-Internet page Retargeting: Advertisements displayed to customers who visited explicit pages on your site.
-Search Retargeting: Focusing on people in light of their internet search tool action, like important catchphrases or questions.
-Email Retargeting: Utilizing email campaigns to reconnect customers who deserted their shopping baskets or perused items without buying.

Changing Abandoned Carts into Sales

Shopping basket deserting is quite possibly one of the most well-known challenges in online business. Retargeting offers an answer by reminding customers to finish their buys.

1. Customized Carts Updates

Send follow-up emails or show promotions exhibiting the particular things left in the truck. Adding an individual touch, for example, tending to the customer by name, can increment commitment.

2. Boost Consummation

Offering a rebate, free transportation, or a restricted time arrangement can rouse customers to finish their buy. For instance:
- "Complete your buy in something like 24 hours and get 10% off!"
- "Just 3 things left in stock — purchase now!"

3. Give Social Confirmation

Feature reviews or evaluations of the items in the truck to build up the worth of the things. Social confirmation can console reluctant consumers and push them toward finishing the exchange.

4. Numerous Retargeting Touchpoints

Utilize a blend of emails, show promotions, and social media promotions to reconnect with the customer across platforms. Reliable openness improves the probability of change.

Tools and Platforms for Successful Retargeting

A few devices and platforms have some expertise in making and managing retargeting efforts. Choosing the right ones can smooth out the cycle and further develop results.

1. Google Advertisements

Google's retargeting platform utilizes the Google Show Organization to show advertisements across a large number of sites. Its extensive reach ensures that your promotions are viewed by a broad audience.

2. Facebook and Instagram Advertisements

These platforms give vigorous retargeting choices, permitting you to draw in customers in light of their communications with your internet-based entertainment pages or site. Custom Audiences are an especially strong element for arriving at past guests.

3. Email Marketing Platforms

Devices like Klaviyo and Mailchimp empower email retargeting via computerizing follow-up crusades. They coordinate with your e-commerce platform to make customized emails for deserted trucks or item suggestions.

4. Dynamic Promotion Platforms

Dynamic promotions, for example, those presented by Facebook or Google, consequently pull item data from your index to make customized advertisements. These promotions are especially successful for retargeting because they show items that customers have previously shown interest in.

5. Outsider Retargeting Devices

Platforms like AdRoll and Criteo represent considerable authority in retargeting efforts. They offer high-level elements, for example, cross-platform retargeting and simulated intelligence-driven streamlining.

Making Compelling Retargeting Efforts

A top-notch retargeting effort requires cautious preparation and insightful performance.

1. Characterize Your Objectives

E-Commerce

-Is your objective to recuperate deserted trucks, drive rehash buys, or increment brand mindfulness?
-Adjust your mission targets to quantifiable results.

2. Section Your Audience
-Not all site guests are similar. Fragment your audience in view of their way of behaving, for example,
-Guests who pursued however didn't add things to the truck.
-Consumers who deserted their trucks.
-Rehash customers who haven't bought in some time.

3. Design Engaging Advertisements
-Utilize convincing visuals and clear suggestions to take action (CTAs).
-Incorporate desperation with phrases like "Restricted Time Proposition" or "Shop Now."
-Feature the advantages or remarkable highlights of your items.

4. Test and Improve
A/B test your retargeting promotions to figure out which plans, CTAs, or offers perform best. Persistently refine your campaigns in light of performance information.

5. Set Recurrence Covers
Abstain from overpowering your audience by restricting the times they see your advertisements. Such a large number of impressions can prompt promotion weakness and diminish viability.

The Effect of Retargeting On Sales and return for Capital Invested
Retargeting has a demonstrated history of expanding sales and conveying serious areas of strength for an on venture (return for capital invested).

1. Higher Commitment Rates
Retargeting advertisements are bound to be tapped on contrasted with conventional showcase promotions since they target customers currently acquainted with your brand.

2. Expanded Change Rates
Reconnecting warm leads guarantees that more guests convert into paying customers, further developing your general sales pipe productivity.

3. Further developed return on initial capital investment
Since retargeting centers around customers further along the consumer's journey, it frequently yields a superior return for capital invested contrasted with cold effort crusades.

4. Improved Customer Bits of knowledge
Following customer conduct through retargeting gives significant information on customer inclinations and buying designs, which can illuminate your more extensive advertising strategy.

Normal Retargeting Difficulties AND Solutions

1. Promotion Weariness

At the point when customers see a similar promotion more than once, they might become irritated or overlook it.

Solutions: Pivot your advertisements oftentimes and present new creatives or offers.

2. Protection Concerns

Consumers are progressively mindful of information protection issues and may feel awkward with excessively customized advertisements.

Solutions: Be straightforward about information utilization and give choices to quit retargeting efforts.

3. Budget Requirements

Retargeting can be costly on the off chance that not overseen cautiously.

Solutions: Begin with a little spending plan, monitor results, and scale fruitful campaigns.

Retargeting and remarketing techniques are important for changing over reluctant consumers, expanding sales, and augmenting the lifetime worth of your customers. By utilizing these methods really, your E-commerce can flourish in a serious market.

CHAPTER 14: BUILDING LONG-TERM CONSUMER LOYALTY

Long-term customer dedication is the foundation of feasible business success. Faithful customers produce reliable income as well as go about as brand ministers, supporting your business and adding to its development. This part looks into procedures to cultivate enduring connections with your customers by zeroing in on excellent help, utilizing steadfastness projects, and building areas of strength for a local area.

Giving Outstanding Customer care

Outstanding customer care is the underpinning of customer reliability. At the point when organizations focus on their customers' necessities and surpass assumptions, they make a enduring impression that cultivates trust and rehashes commitment.

1. Understanding Customer Needs
Undivided attention: Focus on what customers are talking about, both straightforwardly and through input channels, to all the more likely comprehend their inclinations, trouble spots, and assumptions.
-Personalization: Design your communications and contributions to meet individual customer needs. This could range from customized emails to revised item proposals.

2. Consistency Across Touchpoints
Consistent Encounters: Guarantee that customers get a similar degree of value and administration across all channels, whether on the internet, coming up, or through customer assistance.
-Proactive Communication: Keep customers informed about their orders, new contributions, or strategy changes to lessen rubbing and construct trust.

3. Engaging Bleeding Edge Workers
Equip your customer support team with the information and tools they need to effectively resolve issues.
-Urge representatives to take responsibility for worries and resolve them without superfluous administration.

4. Answering Issues with Compassion
-Quick Goal: Address grievances or issues expeditiously to limit disappointment.
-Genuine Statements of regret: Recognize botches sincerely and offer significant arrangements like discounts, substitutions, or limits.
-Exceeding everyone's expectations: Little signals like transcribed cards to say thanks or follow up calls can transform a disappointed customer into a dependable promoter.

E-Commerce

Extraordinary customer support holds customers as well as separates your business in aggressive business sectors, laying the preparation for devotion.

Utilizing Loyalty Programs Hold Customers

Dedication programs are a powerful method for empowering rehash business and developing customer commitment. By offering unmistakable advantages, organizations can create a feeling of significant worth and appreciation, reinforcing the bond with their customers.

1. Planning Successful Dedication Projects
Figure out Customer Inspirations: Direct studies or break down information to figure out what motivators reverberate with your audience.
-Keep It Basic: A direct program with clear rewards and a simple to-explore framework expands investment and fulfillment.
-Offer Significant Prizes: Guarantee that the advantages, whether limits, free items, or select encounters, line up with your customer's inclinations.

2. Kinds of Reliability Projects
Point-Based Frameworks: Customers procure focuses for buys, which they can recover for remunerations.
-Layered Projects: Make various degrees of remunerations to support higher spending or commitment.
-Reference Motivations: Prize customers for getting new business, creating a mutual benefit for the two players.
-Selective Participations: Offer premium advantages, like early admittance to items or free transportation, for a membership charge.

3. Coordinating Innovation for a Consistent Encounter
Use applications or customer entrances to follow rewards, offer customized promotions, and make reclamation bother-free.
-Leverage information examination to recognize drifts and refine program contributions.

4. Measuring Success
Monitor measurements, for example, customer standards for dependability, program support, and income created by dedicated individuals.
-Consistently request feedback to recognize regions for development and keep the program new and locked in.
-When carried out actually, faithfulness programs boost rehash buys as well as cultivate a profound association among customers and your brand.

Making a People Group Around Your Brand

E-Commerce

Incorporating a local area changes customers into advocates who feel associated with your brand past the items or administrations you offer. A strong local area encourages devotion, trust and commitment, giving an upper hand in the present market.

1. Fostering a Brand Character that Resounds
Characterize Your Main Goal and Values: Obviously, articulate what your brand depends on and impart it reliably across all channels.
-Validness Matters: Show certifiable obligation to your qualities through activities, like supporting social causes or keeping up with moral strategic policies.

2. Cultivating Commitment
Make Spaces for Connection: Use virtual entertainment platforms, gatherings, or restrictive gatherings where customers can share encounters and thoughts.
-Energize Customer Created Content: Boost customers to share photographs, testimonials, or reviews connected with your items or administrations.
-Have Occasions: Coordinate face-to-face or virtual occasions like studios, online classes, or meetups to reinforce local area ties.

3. Engaging Brand Diplomats
Distinguish faithful customers who effectively advance your brand and award their support with select advantages or acknowledgment.
-Team up with influencers whose values line up with your brand to intensify your message.

4. Giving Instructive and Worth Driven Content
Offer internet sites, recordings, or bulletins that give experiences, tips, or motivation applicable to your audience.
-Lay out your brand as an expert in your industry by sharing master exhortation and industry patterns.

5. Observing Success Together
Perceive critical accomplishments or commemorations with your local area. This could include extraordinary offers, sellouts, or selective products.
-Share your brand's process, including difficulties and triumphs, to make a story customer can connect with.
-Making a local area encourages a feeling of having a place and guarantees customers feel esteemed, transforming conditional connections into persevering through organizations.

The Effect of Dependability on Business Development
1. Expanded Customer Maintenance

Steadfast customers are less inclined to change to contenders and bound to take part in recurrent buys.

2. Higher Lifetime Worth

A drawn-out customer creates more income over the long run, lessening the need to zero in exclusively on customer procurement.

3. Free Informal Marketing

Steadfast customers frequently become energetic backers, prescribing your business to loved ones.

4. Upgraded Brand Notoriety

A dependable customer base ponders emphatically your business, drawing in new customers and opportunities.

5. Worked on Functional Proficiency

Fulfilled customers need less help and are more sympathetic to intermittent slip-ups, permitting organizations to assign assets more.

By joining excellent customer care, very much planned dedication programs, and a flourishing brand local area, organizations can develop long-term connections that drive development and success. At the point when customers feel esteemed and associated, they are bound to remain faithful, advocate for your brand, and add to its continuous advancement.

Part 5: Scaling Your E-commerce Business

CHAPTER 15: ANALYZING METRICS AND KPIS

In the unique universe of e-commerce, understanding and utilizing measurements and key performance indicators (KPIs) is basic to support success. Measurements uncover the strength of your business, while KPIs give noteworthy bits of knowledge to refine strategies and accomplish explicit objectives. By zeroing in on fundamental e-commerce measurements, utilizing viable devices, and pursuing information-driven choices, organizations can improve activities and lift benefits.

Understanding Key E-commerce Measurements

Measurements are the foundation of performance examination, offering experiences into customer conduct, marketing viability, and generally business wellbeing. Here are the most vital E-commerce measurements to follow:

1. Conversion Rate (CR)
Definition: The level of site guests who complete an ideal activity, like making a buy or pursuing a bulletin.
-Importance: A high change rate demonstrates that your site draws in guests and drives sales.
-Improvement Techniques: Enhance internet architecture, work on the checkout interaction, and proposition convincing suggestions to take action (CTAs).

2. Profit from Investment (return for money invested)
Definition: A proportion of the benefit of your marketing and functional endeavors, determined as (Income - Cost) ÷ Cost.
-Importance: Tracks the viability of campaigns and helps allocate assets to high-performing drives.
-Improvement Systems: Refine focusing on, lessen superfluous consumptions, and spotlight on crusades with demonstrated returns.

3. Customer Lifetime Value (CLV)
Definition: The complete income a business hopes to procure from a solitary customer over their relationship with the brand.
-Importance: CLV accentuates long-term benefits and informs systems to improve customer maintenance.
-Improvement Techniques: Put resources into reliability programs, offer remarkable support, and upsell corresponding items.

4. Bob Rate

E-Commerce

Definition: The level of guests who leave your site without making any move.
Importance: Demonstrates expected issues with site content, plan, or stacking speed.
Improvement Strategies: Upgrade site speed, make drawing in greeting pages, and guarantee portable streamlining.

4. Cart Abandonment Rate
Definition: The level of customers who add things to their truck but neglect to finish the buy.
Importance: Features grating focuses on the buying system.
Improvement Strategies: Work on checkout, offer different installment choices, and send follow-up emails with limits.

5. Average Order Value (AOV)
Definition: The typical sum spent by customers per exchange, determined as Complete Income ÷ Number of Requests.
Importance: Demonstrates the viability of upselling and strategically pitching strategies.
Improvement Procedures: Group items, offer free delivery limits, and suggest related things.

Consistently tracking these measurements allows organizations to understand performance trends and identify growth opportunities.

Instruments FOR Following and Examining Performance

The right apparatuses are fundamental for get-together, sorting out, and deciphering online business information. Here are the absolute best apparatuses for following and examining measurements:

1. Google Examination
Abilities: Tracks site traffic, customer conduct, and transformation rates.
Benefits: Thorough experience in customer socioeconomics, traffic sources, and performance of individual pages.

2. Customer Relationship Management (CRM) Programming
Models: Salesforce, HubSpot.
Abilities: Tracks customer connections, oversees leads and monitors CLV.
Benefits: Assists organizations with keeping up areas of strength for with and grasp customer inclinations.

3. Online business Platforms with Worked in Examination
Models: Shopify, WooCommerce, BigCommerce.
Capacities: Gives sales information, stock following, and customer conduct bits of knowledge.
Benefits: Unified investigation custom-made to online stores.

4. Heatmap Devices

-Models: Hotjar, Insane Egg.
-Capacities: Pictures customer communications with site components, like snaps and parchment.
-Benefits: Distinguishes areas of high and low commitment, helping with site advancement.

5. Social Media Investigation Devices
-Models: Hootsuite, Fledgling Social.
-Abilities: Measures commitment, reach, and return for money invested in internet-based entertainment crusades.
-Benefits: Refines procedures for building brand mindfulness and driving traffic.

6. Email Marketing Platforms
-Models: Mailchimp, Klaviyo.
-Capacities: Tracks open rates, navigates rates, and transformations from email crusades.
-Benefits: Assesses the viability of email marketing endeavors.

7. A/B Testing Devices
-Models: Optimizely, VWO.
-Capacities: Looks at two renditions of an internet site page or marketing resource to figure out which performs better.
-Benefits: Gives information-driven bits of knowledge to streamline change rates.

By utilizing these apparatuses, organizations can acquire significant experiences and monitor progress toward their objectives.

Settling on Information-Driven Choices

Information is just pretty much as important as the activities it illuminates. Pursuing information-driven choices empowers organizations to distinguish qualities, address shortcomings, and gain opportunities. This is the way to successfully utilize information to direct your strategies:

1. Lay out Clear Objectives
Characterize quantifiable goals, for example, expanding change rates, diminishing truck surrender or helping CLV.
-Adjust measurements and KPIs to these objectives to guarantee centered examination.

2. Section Your Information
Separate information by customer socioeconomics, buy history, or traffic sources to uncover explicit examples.
-Use division to customize marketing endeavors and further develop customer encounters.

3. Recognize Patterns and Examples

Search for repeating ways of behaving or performance shifts after some time.
-Figure out which campaigns, items, or channels yield the best outcomes.

4. Test and Enhance Techniques
Utilize A/B testing to try different things with changes, for example, new CTAs or site designs.
-Investigate results to carry out strategies that reliably convey improved results.

5. Follow up on Experiences
For instance, if a high truck deserting rate is distinguished, smooth out the checkout cycle or present updates with motivations.
-Assuming internet-based entertainment commitment is low, change the content system to line up with audience inclinations.

6. Monitor Progress Consistently
Routinely review measurements to guarantee techniques stay successful and adjust to advertise changes.
-Set up mechanized cautions to advise you of huge changes in performance.

7. Embrace Prescient Investigation
Use instruments that break down verifiable information to estimate future patterns and customer ways of behaving.
-Expect customer needs and economic situations to remain in front of the opposition.
   Pursuing informed choices in light of information guarantees that assets are designated successfully and endeavors line up with business objectives.

The Worth of Measurements and KPIS in E-commerce Success
   Examining measurements and KPIs is certainly not a one-time action yet a continuous interaction that develops close by your business. At the point when organizations comprehend their information and use it decisively, they can accomplish:
1. Further developed Customer Encounters
Information uncovers what customers esteem, empowering custom-fitted encounters that drive fulfillment and reliability.
2. Expanded Benefit
Measurements guide endeavors to advance marketing spend, decrease costs, and boost income.
3. Upgraded Functional Effectiveness
Distinguishing bottlenecks and shortcomings takes into account smoothed out cycles and better asset designation.
4. More grounded Strategic advantage
Organizations that follow up on information experiences are defter and better prepared to adjust to advertise patterns.

By becoming amazing at following and investigating measurements and KPIs, E-commerce organizations can open their maximum capacity, driving development and guaranteeing long-term success.

CHAPTER 16: EXPANDING YOUR PRODUCT LINE

Expanding your product offering is a crucial strategy for business development, permitting you to meet advancing customer needs, increment income, and enhance your contributions. Nonetheless, effective extension requires key preparation and cautious performance. This section investigates the vital contemplations for deciding when and how to present new items, techniques for testing thoughts with negligible gamble, and strategies for staying away from the entanglements of over-development.

When and How to Add New Items

The choice to grow your product offering ought to be directed by an intensive examination of your ongoing business sector, customer inclinations, and business capacities. Adding new items with impeccable timing and in the correct manner can fundamentally improve your brand's allure and benefit.

Markers That Now is the Right Time to Extend

1. Steady Customer Feedback

-Assuming that customers as often as possible solicit explicit items or express a need that your ongoing contributions don't meet, it could be an ideal opportunity to investigate those opportunities.
-Monitor reviews, internet-based entertainment remarks, and customer reviews for repeating topics.

2. Market Interest and Patterns

-Recognize holes on the lookout or exploit arising patterns inside your specialty.
-Use instruments like Google Patterns, industry reports, and contender investigation to approve requests.

3. Leveling Sales Development

-In the event that your current product offering has arrived at its development potential, presenting new items can revive sales.
-Search for integral things that line up with your brand and appeal to your interest group.

4. Functional Preparation

-Guarantee your inventory network, creation abilities, and dissemination channels can uphold extra items.
-Consider whether you have the assets to actually advertise and convey new things.

Moves toward Adding New Items

E-Commerce

1. Characterize Your Objectives
Lay out clear goals, for example, expanding a piece of the pie, arriving at another customer portion or supporting normal request esteem.

2. Lead Market research
Evaluate your rivals' contributions, distinguish customer trouble spots, and decide on pricing techniques.
-Investigate your interest group to figure out their inclinations and buying conduct.

3. Begin with Center Skills
-Center around items that line up with your current aptitude and assets.
-Venture into regions where you can use your brand's standing and assets.

4. Foster an Item Guide
-Plan the course of events, creation necessities, and marketing techniques for your new item send-off.
-Set quantifiable success to follow progress and change on a case-by-case basis.

5. Speak with Your Customers
-Produce fervor by including your customers in the process through sneak looks, surveys, or pre-orders.
-Feature how the new item tends to their necessities and improves their experience.

Testing New Ideas with Minimal Risk
Sending off another item generally implies some degree of hazard, however testing thoughts before full-scale performance can relieve possible misfortunes. Here are demonstrated techniques to approve new ideas without overcommitting assets:

1. Market Reviews and Customer Input
-Use reviews, center gatherings, or social media surveys to measure interest in your proposed item
-Connect straightforwardly with your main interest group to refine your thoughts in light of their feedback.

2. Model Testing
-Foster an insignificant suitable item (MVP) to test usefulness and assemble input.
-Offer models to a little gathering of faithful customers or influencers for assessment.

3. Pre-Orders
-Send off a pre-request mission to quantify requests before putting resources into creation.

Use audience funding platforms like Kickstarter or your E-commerce site to produce buzz and secure subsidizing.

Restricted Deliveries
Introduce the item to a particular portion of your audience or in select business sectors.
Break down sales information and customer responses to refine your contribution before a more extensive delivery.

A/B Testing
Try different things with various forms of the item or advertising emails to figure out what reverberates best with your audience.
Use examination instruments to look at performance measurements and settle on informed choices.

Team up with Accomplices
Cooperate with corresponding brands or influencers to test your item in a cooperative mission.
Leverage their audience's bits of knowledge to arrive at new customers and approve your idea.

Staying Away from Over-Development Entanglements
While growing your product offering offers critical advantages, it additionally accompanies chances. Over-extension can strain assets, weaken your brand, and overpower customers. This is the way to keep away from normal traps:

Keep up with Brand Consistency
Guarantee that new items line up with your brand identity, values, and customer assumptions.
Try not to present things that are in contention with your current contributions or befuddle your main interest group.

Center around Higher expectations without compromise
Focus on conveying great items instead of sending off numerous things at the same time.
A more modest, well-organized product offering frequently resounds more with customers than an excessively wide determination.

Oversee Stock Astutely
Abstain from overloading new items before testing interest.
Use stock administration frameworks to follow sales and forestall pointless storing.

Dispense Assets Decisively
Evaluate the monetary and functional effect of presenting new items.
Try not to extend your budget or group limit excessively dainty.

5. Monitor Performance Measurements
-Routinely assess the sales and benefits of every item in your extended line.
-Suspend failing to meet expectations to zero in on top-selling items.

6. Pay attention to Customer Input
-Constantly assemble feedback to recognize likely issues and work on your contributions.
-Fabricate trust by tending to worries instantly and straightforwardly.

The Advantages OF Key Item Development
When executed mindfully, growing your product offering can yield critical benefits for you business:

1. Expanded Income
-New items give extra income streams and draw in new customer sections.
2. Improved Customer Steadfastness
-Addressing a greater amount of your customers' requirements cultivates steadfastness an supports rehash buys.
3. More grounded Market Position
-A different product offering can separate your brand and fortify your upper hand.
4. Worked on Functional Proficiency
-Utilizing existing foundations for new items can amplify asset use.
5. Manageable Development
-Progressive, key development guarantees long-term accomplishment without overburdening you business.

Expanding your product offering is both an open door and an obligation. By surveying marke interest, testing ideas, and avoiding overdevelopment, you can ensure that each new produc strengthens your brand and contributes to sustainable growth. Smart performance will allow you business to evolve and meet the ever-changing needs of your customers.

CHAPTER 17: EXPLORING INTERNATIONAL MARKETS

Venturing into global business sectors is an intriguing learning experience for E-commerce organizations, offering admittance to new customer bases and expanded income potential. Notwithstanding, entering a global market likewise accompanies difficulties that require cautious preparation and variation. In this section, we will investigate the advantages and obstructions of selling universally, procedures for fitting your store to global audiences, and best practices for managing coordinated factors, expenses, and guidelines.

Difficulties and Advantages of Selling Globally

Selling globally opens ways to a universe of chances, yet it likewise expects organizations to explore new intricacies. Understanding the difficulties and advantages can assist you with planning for progress.

The Advantages of Global Development

1. Admittance to New Customers
-Expanding past homegrown lines permits you to take advantage of developing business sectors with more popularity for your items.
-Various business sectors offer chances to arrive at undiscovered socioeconomics.

2. Expanded Income Potential
-By selling globally, you can broaden your income streams and decrease dependence on a solitary market.
-Occasional interest varieties in various nations assist with adjusting sales over time.

3. Improved Brand Recognition
-A global presence helps your brand's believability and positions it as a market chief.
-Expanded visibility in global business sectors reinforces your standing and opens entryways for joint efforts.

4. Upper hand
-Expanding universally permits you to remain in front of contenders who presently can't seem to enter global business sectors.
-Laying out early traction in developing business sectors sets out long-term opportunities for development.

The Difficulties of Global Expansion

1. Social and Language Boundaries
-Adjusting to local customs, dialects, and shopper conduct requires examination and responsiveness.
-False impressions or social cold-heartedness can hurt your brand's standing.

E-Commerce

2. Strategies and Delivery Intricacies
-Managing global transportation, customs, and conveyance timetables can challenge.
-High transportation expenses might affect evaluating and net revenues.

3. Administrative Consistency
-Exploring different duty regulations, import/send out guidelines and exchange approaches adds intricacy.
-Inability to agree with nearby guidelines can bring about fines or functional interruptions.

4. Currency and Installment or Payment Issues
-Offering numerous installment strategies and taking care of cash transformations might require extra assets.
-Conversion scale variances can leverage productivity.

Adjusting Your Store for Global Audiences
Fitting your e-commerce store to address the issues of global customers is pivotal for progress. This includes tending to language, social inclinations, and customer experience.

1. Restriction
-Make an interpretation of your site into the dialects of your objective business sectors to make route and buying more straightforward.
-Utilize proficient interpretation administrations to guarantee exactness and social significance.
2. Social Awareness
-Adjust item portrayals, symbolism, and marketing efforts to align with local customs and inclinations.
-Try not to utilize brands, varieties, or expressions that might convey accidental implications in various societies.
3. Currency and Installment/Payment Choices
-Offer local money evaluation to improve straightforwardness and trust.
-Incorporate district-explicit installment techniques, such as digital wallets, charge cards, or bank moves.
4. Adaptable Transportation Choices
-Give a scope of transportation choices, from standard to expedited service, to address different customer needs.
-Obviously, impart assessed conveyance times and transportation costs.
5. Advance for Mobile Customers
-Guarantee your site is dynamic, as numerous global customers depend on cell phones for internet-based shopping.
-Utilize responsive plan and quick stacking pages to upgrade customer experience.

5. Global Customer service
-Offer multilingual customer service to address inquiries and resolve issues instantly.
-Give clear and available return and discount approaches customized to global exchanges.

Managing Strategies, Expenses, AND Guidelines

Effectively dealing with strategies, charges, and administrative necessities is fundamental for consistent global tasks.

Coordinated factors

1. Pick Strong Transportation Accomplices
-Band together with laid-out messenger administrations experienced in global transportation.
-Search for choices that give following, protection, and customs support.
2. Customs Documentation
-Ensure that all shipments are accompanied by accurate traditional notifications to avoid delays.
-Work with strategic suppliers to explore country-explicit prerequisites.
3. Warehousing and Satisfaction
-Think about utilizing outsider coordinated operations (3PL) suppliers or laying out local distribution centers to lessen delivery times and expenses.
-Satisfaction focuses in target locales can improve conveyance proficiency and consumer loyalty.

Taxes and Obligations

1. Understand Tax Obligations
-Research value-added tax (VAT), goods and services tax (GST), and import obligations for your objective business sectors.
-Decide if you want to enroll for charge purposes in every country.

2. Straightforward Pricing
-Show item costs comprehensive of expenses or obligations to keep away from treatment for customers.
-Use charge estimation devices to give precise pricing during checkout.

3. Tax Software Integration
-Coordinate assessment consistency programming with your online business platform to computerize computations and filings.
-Instruments like Avalara or TaxJar work on global expenses on the board.

Administrative Consistency

1. Import and Exports Regulations

-Find out about the import/export limitations and item certificates expected in your objective nations.
-Guarantee your items meet security, marking, and bundling norms.

2. Information Security Guidelines
-Conform information insurance regulations like GDPR (General Information Assurance Guideline) for EU customers.
-Update your protection strategy and guarantee the secure treatment of customer information.

3. Confined Items
-Check for limitations on items like gadgets, food, or beauty care products that might confront extra investigation.

Strategies for Effective Global Expansion
1. Begin Little
-Center around a couple of key business sectors before growing further.
-Utilize your underlying development as a growth opportunity to refine your strategy.

2. Leverage Commercial centers
-Use platforms like Amazon, eBay, or Alibaba to test new business sectors with negligible speculation.
-These platforms offer an inherent foundation for transportation, installments, and customer care.

3. Put resources into Market research
-Persistently monitor market patterns, customer conduct, and contender movement in your objective areas.
-Change your contributions and marketing systems given your experiences.

4. Build Partnerships
-Team up with nearby merchants, influencers, or organizations to fortify your market presence.
-Leverage their skill and organizations to lay out validity.

Investigating global business sectors is a compensating yet complex undertaking. By understanding the difficulties, fitting your way to deal with global audiences, and managing planned operations with accuracy, you can situate your brand for long-term progress in the global commercial center. Extend in a calculated manner, adjust proactively, and leverage the immense opportunities that global business sectors offer.

Conclusion

Expanding e-commerce is a journey that requires key preparation, flexibility, and a promise of constant development. All through this book, we have investigated the fundamental components of building a fruitful internet-based store, from understanding your audience and making convincing item postings to dominating marketing, examining performance measurements, and scaling universally. Every part has given noteworthy techniques to assist you with exploring difficulties, taking advantage of chances, and streamlining your tasks.

Key focus points incorporate the significance of conveying outstanding customer encounters, utilizing information-driven bits of knowledge, and keeping an unmistakable vision for your brand. The outcome in e-commerce isn't about alternate routes; it's tied in with building trust, cultivating faithfulness, and remaining in front of advancing patterns.

Presently, it's your chance to make a move. Execute the strategies illustrated in this book to develop your business bit by bit. Embrace the difficulties as learning opportunities and stay zeroed in on your drawn-out objectives. Whether you're simply beginning or scaling higher than ever, the devices and bits of knowledge shared here will engage you to flourish in the serious universe of online business.

Your process doesn't end here — it starts. Remain motivated, continue to develop, and watch your business thrive on the global platform. The fate of your e-commerce success is in your grasp.

www.ingramcontent.com/pod-product-compliance
Lightning Source LLC
Chambersburg PA
CBHW071110240526
45469CB00006BD/2421